4WD & HAND HELD

GPS

FRED STUDDEN & ANDREW MONROE

First published 2012

Published and distributed by
Australian Fishing Network
PO Box 544 Croydon, Victoria 3136
Telephone: (03) 9729 8788 Facsimile: (03) 9729 7833
Email: sales@afn.com.au
Website: www.afn.com.au

©Australian Fishing Network 2012

ISBN: 9781 8651 3191 7

CONTENTS

However you choose to go off road, it's always advisable to have a GPS with you.

INTRODUCTION

The Global Position System (GPS) has changed all types of navigation across the world, simplifying and improving the accuracy of finding our way around, no matter where we want to go and no matter what terrain we may encounter.

More importantly, GPS technology enables us to know almost exactly where we are, no matter where we may be travelling – in the middle of the Simpson Desert, alongside a rainforest river in Cape York or amongst the tall timber of the Victorian high country.

Understanding the technicalities of this system is not strictly necessary to be able to use a GPS unit, or to find your way safely around in strange surroundings, or to pinpoint exactly where you are. However, knowledge of the basics should make the learning process quicker and more enjoyable. The first section of the book explains the basics of GPS, whereas later sections get more 'hands-on' and hardware focussed.

As well as background knowledge of how GPS works, it is important to become familiar with using your GPS unit. As always, practice makes perfect and the more you use your GPS before you really need to do so, the better the outcome when you come to rely on it. Don't leave your GPS in its box; use it at every opportunity (even if it is not really necessary to do so) and make sure that you become fluent at making this handy device earn its keep. Getting other people in your group to become familiar with how to use the GPS will also be beneficial.

Since GPS was originally designed and used for marine navigation, much of the GPS terminology (jargon) is directly related to the nautical language of navigation. Fortunately, you only need to know a few of these terms to come to grips with the system, and once you understand them, the whole system becomes second nature.

Throughout the text, when GPS terminology is used, its meaning will be explained. However, I have not dwelt on the fine points of GPS technology, but more on the practicalities of using a GPS and getting the best out of your purchase.

Good navigating!

Andrew Monroe

GLOBAL POSITIONING SYSTEM (GPS)

The Global Positioning System (GPS) is a satellite based navigation system using radio signals from a series of orbiting satellites. On the ground, each GPS unit records the signals it receives and, since each satellite has a unique identifier (signal) and since not all satellites will be in view at any one time, it can then calculate where on the surface of planet earth the GPS unit is located.

The Global Positioning System consists of 28 satellites in a high orbit, some 20,000 kilometres above the earth's surface. The satellites are maintained by the US military, and were until recently the only satellite based navigation system available (alternative systems are being established by Russia, China and the European Union).

The orbits are designed to guarantee at least four satellites are always in view, at every point on the earth's surface, twenty four hours a day (there are exceptions to this in the high polar regions). However, in many instances as many as twelve or thirteen satellites will be visible. Each satellite in the constellation orbits the earth twice a day, and each satellite continually transmits a radio signal, which contains a coded sequence of numbers, unique to each satellite. This signal identifies:

- the satellite (by its number).
- its position in the satellite constellation.
- a precise time signal using UTC (Universal Time Coordinates, formerly known as Greenwich Mean Time).
- position and orbit data of all the other satellites in the constellation (this is sometimes referred to as 'almanac' data).

GPS UNITS

A GPS Unit (also known as a GPS Receiver, the part of the GPS system you use) does not transmit any signals, it only receives radio signals from the satellites that are radio visible to the GPS (that is, in direct line of sight of the GPS).

The receiver measures the time of arrival of each signal, and thereby calculates the range (distance) of each satellite. Once the range of the satellites is known, the position of the receiver can be determined by triangulation. If it were possible to measure 'true satellite range' directly, it would only be necessary to track data from two satellites to obtain the receivers latitude and longitude. This range measurement depends on accurately measuring the time taken for the radio signal, which is travelling at the speed of light, to reach the receiver. Unfortunately, the satellite transmissions are affected by the earth's outer atmosphere, as well as timing errors in the satellite clock and in the GPS receiver's own internal clock. To correct these errors, a minimum of three satellites are required to obtain an initial fix.

Graphic illustration of the satellite positions and satellites being used for the fix. This display is generally shown immediately on start-up.

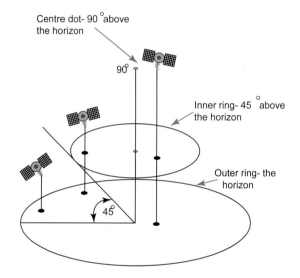

Centre dot- 90° above the horizon

90°

Inner ring- 45° above the horizon

Outer ring- the horizon

45°

Satellite Sky View

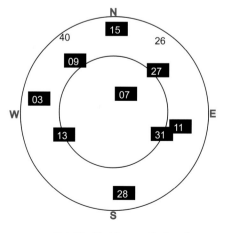

Satellite Sky View as displayed in the GPS Information Page

When a GPS receiver is first turned on, the unit's antenna receives signals from all of the satellites that are 'visible' (visible in this sense refers to satellites' signals that are able to reach the receiver's antenna in a straight line-of-sight). If a radio opaque material such as metal or masonry is between the receiver's antenna and the satellite, this will partially block the radio signal. For this reason, GPS reception in buildings generally varies from poor to non-existent. Also, heavy foliage such as trees can impede reception of the satellite signals, particularly if the foliage is wet. Fortunately, glass does not block radio signals, so GPS receivers may be used successfully inside vehicles, receiving the radio signal through the windscreen. Almost all in-car navigators depend on signal reception through windscreen glass.

To further improve the overall accuracy of the GPS systems particularly for aviation navigation and especially for planes operating in conditions of poor visibility from smaller airports that do not support instrument landing, several enhancement systems have come on line in the last few years. The North American system is called Wide Area Augmentation System (WAAS) and the European equivalent is European Geostationary Navigation Overlay Service (EGNOS).

Most GPS receivers now have the capability to receive and process these additional correction signals, but the present GPS system generally offers accuracy of about five metres – and often considerably better than this – which is more than adequate for most applications and certainly is adequate for bushwalking or driving in all but the most extreme weather conditions.

CHOOSING A GPS UNIT

As you would expect, GPS units come in all shapes and sizes, and with a range of features and cost points. Some important things to consider when making your selection include:

Size of the Screen.
GPS units intended for marine application will generally have a large display screen, to make viewing easier in a

boat bumping about on the water. Similarly, a GPS for use in a vehicle will need to have a reasonable sized screen – something like 60 mm x 100 mm (about 130 mm as measured diagonally across the screen).

If you are going 'bush' (for example, on foot or in a canoe) then a smallish hand-held unit such as the Magellan Explorist will be appropriate. Units such as this have a screen of about 50 mm x 70 mm, with some smaller hand-held units having a screen of about 35 mm x 45 mm. Even smaller GPS devices are available from companies such as Suunto, Timex and Tom Tom, who manufacture watches with in-built GPS capability. Unless bulk and weight are a major issue for you, then the 50 mm x 70 mm (approx) size should be regarded as the minimum size as screens smaller than this can become tiresome to use.

Voice Guidance.
If you are choosing a GPS for use in a vehicle, then the unit will usually have a 'voice guidance' option; that is, the unit can provide specific directions using voice based directions as well as a running commentary on road conditions (such as speed limit zones etc). Apparently most of us prefer a female voice for this task, but this is user selectable from the set-up menu. If you find the voice a bit grating, some units (such as selected ones from the NavMan range) have a small FM transmitter that allows you to pipe the voice commands through the vehicle speaker system. Also, some manufacturers provide additional voices for download from their websites. Hand-held units do not normally include the 'voice guidance' feature.

Display Options.
Similar to the 'Voice Guidance' feature, if you are choosing a GPS for use in a vehicle, then the unit will usually have a 'street display' option for the screen output.

The unit can provide a graphic of the roadway as it would appear through the windscreen, with lane markings, signage, city skylines etc as an alternative to the normal 'map and flashing cursor' style of display.

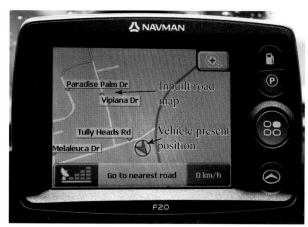

The beauty of GPS units lies in their ability to show you exactly where you are.

Standard Maps

Standard Maps are maps available as a standard feature of the unit; they are also known as 'basemaps'. If you will mainly be on well travelled routes then a unit loaded with standard city and touring route maps will be fine. If you are heading 'off-the-beaten-track' then you should be looking for a set of 4WD rated maps, and/or a set of topographic maps as a standard feature.

Additional Maps

Additional Maps are maps that can be bought as an after-purchase product and then loaded into the unit. There is a limit to the number of maps that can be loaded into the memory of a GPS unit, consequently it may be worth paying extra for the option of being able to load additional maps (via an SD card reader or USB port).

The VMS4x4 (*www.vms4x4.com*), the Hema Navigator (*www.hema.com*) and the MY60T from NavMan (*www. navman.com*) are good choices for additional maps

(and hardware). The VMS unit has the iTOPO range of 1:250 000 scale topographic maps, providing complete coverage of Australia. The Hema Navigator comes pre-loaded with all of the Hema 'outback' maps (the same maps can be loaded onto the SD card of the VMS4x4) and the NavMan unit also utilises the Hema Maps. The 4WD maps produced by Gregorys are also available in digital format, ready for transfer to a GPS.

Similarly, the various state government mapping agencies now have their complete topographic map inventory available in digital format. For example, Victoria is covered by two data files (Victoria East and Victoria West) that cover the entire state at a scale of 1:25 000.

Some units (such as selected ones from the NavMan range) have the ability to use downloadable travel guides (for example, from Lonely Planet), and these provide an extra layer of mapping and other travel information.

Updates.

Maps (particularly city maps) soon get out of date, and the ability of the manufacturer to provide updated maps at periodic intervals (usually via an internet download) may be an important feature to look for. Some manufacturers provide free map updates for a limited time, after which the so-called 'sunset clause' kicks in, and you need to pay for further updates.

Route Selection.

Vehicle based GPS units will have as their main feature, the ability to select a route from one location to another, and then to give verbal instruction en route to guide you on your way. This normally involves selecting a town/ suburb from a list, then a street, then a house number etc. Hand-held GPS do not normally have this feature.

Hibernation (also called 'sleep mode').

Most hand-held GPS units will go into a 'hibernate' mode after a set interval with no buttons pressed, and this is an important battery saving feature. In hibernate mode, the unit will continue to receive and process GPS data from the satellites, but other functions (such as the screen display) are shut down. Obviously, this is not a desirable feature for vehicle based GPS units.

The ability to connect a GPS unit to a PC or laptop enables you to download new and updated maps for the unit.

External Connections (the ability of the unit to communicate with a PC, or similar device).

This normally requires a USB port on the GPS, and will enable you to download new (and updated) maps for the unit, as well as to download GPS waypoint listings for long distance walks and treks from the internet (more of this later).

Operating Conditions.

Waterproof units are handy when going fishing or boating, and dust proof units are handy for the Australian outback if they are going to be used outdoors. Most manufacturers now refer to an IPX number (international standard, IEC 60529) when stating the ability of their units to operate under different conditions (IPX00 has no protection against dust or water ingress, whereas IPX08 can operate under water permanently).

Batteries.

Some GPS units have rechargeable (but not replaceable) batteries, whereas others have non-rechargeable batteries that are easily replaced. The advantage of the former is that you don't need to carry a set of replacement batteries with you, but on the other hand, you do have a constant need for a source of power for recharging. The advantage of the latter is that you are not dependent on having access to a power source for recharging when you are out in remote areas (but, of course, you need to have several sets of batteries with you).

Each manufacturer quotes the expected operational life of the unit's battery system. These figures will be under ideal conditions, such as fresh, new batteries, not using the backlight feature for the display screen etc. For practical and safety reasons, assume that the unit will work for about 80 per cent of the quoted figure.

Many manufacturers recommend taking the batteries out of the unit when you are not going to use it for a while. From hard earned experience, if you leave the batteries in, the chances are that after a few weeks they will be dead flat, whether you have used the unit or not.

External Power.

Marine units will usually receive their power from the boat's main power supply. Similarly, GPS units specifically designed for in-vehicle use will use the vehicle's electrical system for power, either via a 'cigarette lighter' style connector, a USB port on the vehicle's radio fascia or by fixed wiring during manufacture of the vehicle. External power should always be used wherever (and whenever) possible to conserve the internal batteries. Rechargeable batteries (and a portable means of recharging them) are also a useful investment.

If linking your GPS to a computer (or similar device) you will need a GPS unit with a USB port, a USB cable and a computer with a free USB port. Having made the necessary connections, and turned the GPS and computer on, the display on the GPS should offer a range of communication options, and the one designated something like 'Power only' is the one to select.

Method of Mounting.

Many GPS units will be mounted on a car dashboard, but you may need a marine style mounting with a spray cover, or a special bracket for a mountain bike and so on. Ideally, the unit needs to be easily clipped securely into a mounting bracket and equally easily removed when you leave the boat or vehicle unattended for any extended period.

One of the best options when choosing a GPS unit, is to get one that can be used in a variety of circumstances – one with a large enough screen (and secure enough mounting) to be used on the car dashboard, yet small enough (and rugged enough) to take on a bushwalk. The Magellan Explorist 710 is a good choice for this combination of uses, with an excellent range of features such as:

- turn-by-turn instructions for in-car use
- excellent screen display, providing good reading in direct sunlight
- touring maps included as standard
- worldwide base maps included as standard
- topographic maps included as standard
- electronic compass
- barometric altimeter
- fishing calendar
- sun and moon calendar
- 3.2 megapixel camera
- tested to the IPX-7 standard (an extremely rugged unit)
- 500–2000 waypoint capability

The Magellan Explorist 710

As well as dedicated GPS units, many mobile phones can be GPS enabled and these are quite handy as long as you are not venturing too far off-the-beaten-track. The cost (and size) of data downloads can be an issue with this method of using GPS technology. Several manufacturers provide the necessary software to enable the GPS mode in mobiles; see, for example, *www.quickgps.com*.

In a similar vein, several of the 'tablet' style devices (such as the iPad) have a built-in GPS chip and these devices can be used as an alternative to the traditional style GPS units. A major advantage of using such units

is that they have a significantly larger screen than most other options.

PCs are not left out of the action here, with several manufacturers (such as Garmin) having a GPS 'mouse', a device that you plug into a USB port and then clip onto the exterior of a vehicle (the 'clip' is usually a magnet). Once loaded up, a GPS mouse provides the usual GPS style display on the computer screen, and is an inexpensive way of accessing GPS data. Not all mice are compatible with all GPS enabled maps, so take care in product selection to get the best results from this option.

A few points about GPS units compared to maps,

- GPS units can stop working, due to poor signals, water damage, chip failure or battery failure; maps are not vulnerable to any of these factors. Non-response of the unit due to poor signals is less of a problem with the newer designs of GPS. If you have problems getting a 'fix' then it may be necessary to move a few hundred metres to get better reception. This may mean getting to a road junction when amongst tall timber, or climbing up a slope from a low point. Reception can be a particular problem in steep-sided river valleys and it is worth remembering that river banks are usually the lowest point in the topography for many kilometres around you.
- Maps are good for trip planning, whilst GPS devices are good for monitoring progress; particularly given their ability to indicate when you have made a wrong turn or are heading in the wrong direction.
- Maps will give an overall image of your surrounds; GPS, with their small screens, are not so useful for this.

- Using a GPS for fundamental route selection is not necessarily a good move as it is unlikely a GPS will be able to select the best (safest and most practicable) route through a particular area. So far, only the logic of a human brain seems capable of doing this, particularly for long and/or complex routes. This is not to say that you should not use a GPS for route selection as if you do not know the area you will be travelling through, then a GPS selected route is probably going to be as good as it gets.
- If you do need to use a GPS for route selection, then it may be useful to set some of the parameters used by

the GPS unit for this task. For example, if you are towing, then selecting 'caravan' or 'truck' from the vehicle type may save you from being sent down a narrow urban street or a gravel road. Similarly, de-selecting 'unsealed roads' can keep you out of the back-blocks. If you are driving a really big rig then a 'truck' focused GPS (such as those produced by ProNav) may be a good investment; see *www.pronav.com.au* for more details.

• In many respects, the GPS is only as good as the maps it uses; if there are errors in the mapping then things could get a little confusing. It is not uncommon in the high country to see the GPS location cursor happily blinking away in the midst of swathes of greenery, or doing the same in vast tracks of sand in the outback, with not a single road or track being displayed on the map. However, regardless of this occurrence, the GPS will still tell you where you are, and this will enable you to maintain a 'sense of place' and to pinpoint your location on a map.

• Having a GPS does not reduce your dependency on being able to read a map. Whether you are looking at the screen of a GPS unit and/or looking at a map, you will still need to be able to relate what you are seeing on the screen (or on paper) with your surrounds.

Finally, do you need a GPS? For most travellers, the answer is yes. A GPS gives an added veneer of safety to all of your travel, particularly since it will provide accurate monitoring of your position and progress.

Do you need to carry a spare GPS? Not necessarily, but it is helpful to have a small hand-held waterproof unit (such as a Magellan Triton) on your travels. In this way there is always a standby in case there are problems with the vehicle mounted unit, and if you want to get out on some walking tracks there is a nice, compact waterproof (and therefore dustproof) GPS to help you on your way.

On a legal note, it appears that it is permissible to use a GPS whilst driving, providing it is enclosed in a professionally designed and manufactured housing fixed to the vehicle in some way. This implies that it is not legal to use a small hand unit (such as those favoured by bushwalkers) whilst driving (most state motoring authorities agree on this point). The same administrators say that the best place for a GPS is low down and to the right of the driver; my preference is to the left of the driver and high up near the rear vision mirror, since this enables other passengers to see the screen and for the front seat passenger to call up data and to create waypoints etc. If you mount the GPS left of the driver and low down on the windscreen, there may be legal issues regarding forward visibility.

FEATURES OF GPS UNITS

As mentioned earlier, a full A-Z understanding of GPS is not strictly necessary to use these devices, although some knowledge is desirable. However, understanding the main operational features of your GPS unit is important to maximise the value you get from the unit.

Location.

The main feature of the GPS system is that it can tell you exactly where you are on the surface of the earth. This position is known as a fix, and the accuracy of the fix will vary slightly depending on the relative positions of the satellites at the time of the fix, but is generally between five and ten metres. Your position will be expressed either in the traditional latitude and longitude coordinates or in UTM (Universal Transverse Mercator) coordinates. A full explanation of these coordinate systems is included later.

Coordinates.

As well as displaying the coordinates of your current location, the GPS can store those coordinates, as well as the coordinates of other documented locations, on your travels.

Speed.

Once having activated your GPS, the unit will continually monitor your speed over each segment of your current journey and calculate your average speed. This is particularly handy if you are in a slow moving mode of transport such as mountain bike in rugged terrain or a 4WD in sand dune country. The maximum speed achieved throughout the days' activities will also be shown on the same screen.

Distance.

Similar to the speed display referred to above, the GPS will also calculate the distance covered during this session (for example, during a particular day of travel), as well as the cumulative distance covered since you last zeroed the 'trip meter'. It is always a good idea to zero the trip meter before commencing each significant journey, as this will help monitor how you are progressing in both time and distance. For example, if you are tackling the Oodnadatta Track, then setting the trip meter to zero at Marree would be appropriate, along with noting the intermediate distances at various landmarks such as Lake Eyre, Coward Springs, William Creek, Algebuckina Bridge and Oodnadatta.

Waypoints.

The ability of a GPS unit to record waypoints (significant places on your route) is one of the most useful aspects of GPS technology. As waypoints, the GPS can store the coordinates of where you are or the coordinates of any other documented locations on your route (see below). These locations (waypoints) are then stored in memory and can be recalled when required. Using a 'Go To' function, the GPS unit can then display the distance and bearing necessary to get back to a particular waypoint from your current location.

On most GPS units, the default data when creating a waypoint is usually the current location, although this can easily be overridden. Ideally, you would create a waypoint at each point where a change of direction occurs and/or there is a road-track junction or some other point of interest.

Routes.

A route is a series of pre-entered waypoints. When the waypoints are linked together they form a route (also known as a route sequence). Like waypoints, this route may be given a name and stored in memory. This route can then be navigated either in the forward direction (that is, following the route in the original direction taken when the waypoints were made) or in the reverse direction to get you back to a previous known location, or back to base.

If you enter the data for the route manually, then a fair amount of effort and accuracy is required, however many popular walking routes and popular 4WD treks have an associated GPX file, which can be downloaded from the internet to a PC and then copied to a GPS unit. See for example, *www.heysentrail.asn.au* (the Heysen Trail is a long distance walking trail in South Australia) and the file shown here, which provides waypoint data (in GPX format) for the Tanami Track in the Northern Territory.

Label	Type	Symbol	Description	Waypoint	Comment	Latitude	Longitude	Elevation
TT_01	1	◈	Stuart Highway	road junction	1100km to go	23.31.58S	133.51.36E	726m
TT_02	2	⊡	Tropic of Capricorn	geographic feature		23.26.26S	133.15.06E	639m
TT_03	3	○	Rest/Camping Area	camp site	lots of room	23.16.16S	132.55.06E	620m
TT_04	1	◈	Gary Junction Road	road junction		23.11.16S	132.50.54E	593m
TT_05	4	✦	Tilmouth Roadhouse	fuel stop	fuel, accommodation etc	22.48.41S	132.35.40E	560m
TT_06	1	◈	Yuendumu t/o	road junction	fuel and store in town	22.16.44S	131.49.00E	719m
TT_07	4	✦	Rabbit Flat Roadhouse	fuel stop	closed down?	20.11.91S	130.01.17E	339m
TT_08	2	⊡	WA/NT border	geographic feature		19.53.28S	129.00.01E	416m
TT_09	3	○	Sturt Creek	camp site	Billiluna close by (fuel)	19.33.11S	127.41.27E	300m
TT_10	1	◈	Wolfe Creek t/o	road junction	turn off to Wolfe Creek	19.10.24S	127.38.49E	354m
TT_11	2	⊡	Wolfe Creek crater	geographic feature	Wolfe Creek Crater	19.10.53S	127.47.25E	351m
TT_12	1	◈	Great Northern Highway	road junction		18.19.29S	127.33.03E	430m

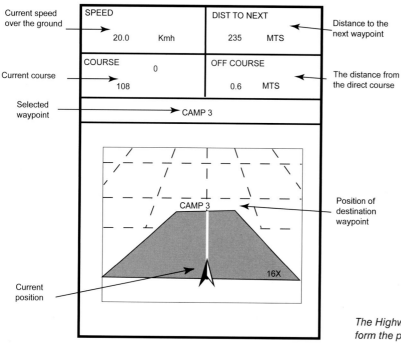

The Highway display indicates in a graphic form the progress towards the waypoint.

Tracks and Trails.

Another important function of the GPS comes into play when the GPS receiver is moving. The GPS can record and store the track actually taken during this movement. The track is also known as a 'trail', 'snail trail' or 'breadcrumb trail' or just simply 'crumbs'. These tracks can be named and stored in the unit's memory and recalled on the unit's screen as required. They can then be used as a method of returning to a previously known position or your original starting position.

If you are using a pre-entered route for your journey, the track may just be a copy of the planned route, but if you deviate from the route (intentionally or otherwise) then the track data will be of more importance than the route data. In GPS jargon, the word track does not necessarily imply a formed pathway or roadway, it is simply a record of where you have been. Track data (as stored by the GPS unit) is of similar format to that of a GPX file.

Route Selection.

Vehicle based GPS units will have as their main feature the ability to select a route from one location to another, and then to give verbal instructions en route to guide you on your way. This normally involves selecting a town/suburb from a list, then a street, then a house number etc. More of this is available under 'In-car GPS Navigators'.

Compass.

The compass screen shows a traditional compass face, with both degrees and compass points designated around the compass rose. The compass screen usually shows the direction of the sun and moon relative to your current position (even though neither may be visible to you). More on the compass screen later.

Compass Display Page

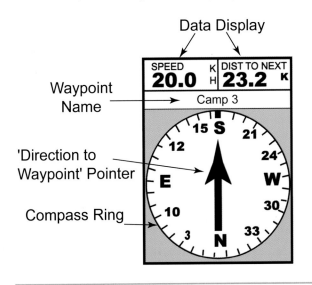

The compass display screen displays a compass card indicating the current direction you are travelling, current speed and distance to next waypoint.

Status.

The status screen shows a graphic of the satellites currently in view, often with graphs showing the strength of the signal being received from each satellite. Some status screens also include messages like 'searching...' when a reliable fix is still in progress.

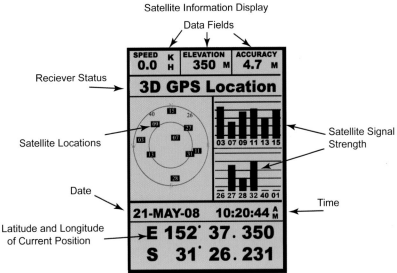

This display provides detailed information of the satellites and the GPS fix.

Since each brand of receiver may vary a little from these descriptions (and accompanying diagrams) you should refer to the instruction manual included with your particular unit for detailed descriptions of the terms used and how your unit works. If you do not have a manual, copies for most of the popular brands and models can be downloaded free of charge from the manufacturers' websites (see Useful Resources at the end of the book).

MAPS and MAP SCALES

Maps used for serious land navigation are generally known as topographic maps as opposed to marine maps, which are known as nautical charts. The most common scales used on topographic maps are 1:250 000, 1:100 000, 1:50 000 and 1:25 000. These maps are produced by state government authorities, and companies that specialise in map production. Some maps contain additional information specifically focusing on activities such as angling, 4WD tracks, bushwalking or simply general tourist information. See the *Useful Resources* section at the back of the book for a comprehensive listing of Australian map publishers.

Regardless of your particular needs for maps whilst in the outback or any remote area, it is important that you carry at least one map of the area you are travelling through. If you are travelling by vehicle this may be a tourist style map of a particular geographical area (for example, the Kimberley Ranges), a map of the entire state (in this case, Western Australia), a series of topographic maps (such as those at a scale of 1:250 000) or just an atlas (a book of maps).

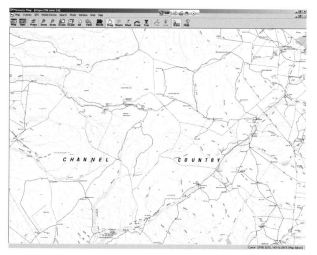

Topographic maps such as this are ideal for serious land navigation.

Most maps produced in the modern era are available in printed and digital format. This means that you can load these maps onto a PC (or similar device) and you can then extract navigation information from these maps – information such as the coordinates of a particular location. The ability to do this requires not only the map in digital format, but some mapping software to read the map data; more of this later.

The amount of detail shown on a map is largely determined by the scale at which features on the ground are represented on paper. The scale on a map is usually represented by numbers such as 1:100 000, 1:150 000, 1:250 000 and 1:400 000 and so on. The greater the number after the colon the less the detail (if you prefer big number = big area covered; small number = small area covered). So whilst a map at a scale of 1:400 000 may be great for a trip along the Tanami Track (Northern Territory), a map at a scale of about 1:25 000 would be required for a walk in Tasmania's Cradle Mountain National Park or other similar remote area.

Large scale maps and an atlas can be used for trip planning and to get an overview of your intended route. If you are staying on the bitumen this is an appropriate level of mapping detail to aim for. If you intend doing some detailed exploration as you travel, then a regional map will help prevent you from going astray and to get the most from your efforts. If your journey involves parking your vehicle and heading off on foot, then some more detail is required.

The most common map scales are 1:250 000, 1:100 000, 1:50 000 or 1:25 000, and (as mentioned above) the larger scale (that is, those with a smaller number after the 1:) gives greater detail, but covers a smaller area while the smaller scale (that is, larger number after the 1:) has less detail, but depicts a greater area. This use of 'larger' and 'smaller' can be confusing! There are several ways of keeping the confusion at bay on this matter; for example, you can say small number = small area = big amount of detail (ssb); whereas big number = big area = small amount of detail (bbs).

Depending on the scale, the grid lines on the map will be spaced at intervals that make up a square grid. Also printed on the border of the map will be a distance scale, shown as a ruler. This can be used to take direct measurements of distance from the map using dividers or a simple rule. Usually it is easier to calculate the relationship between millimetres on the ruler to calculate distance, rather than use dividers. For example, if a particular map has a scale of 1:100 000, then 10 mm measured on the map equals one kilometre. Another way of looking at this is to say that one millimetre is equal to 100 metres.

It is vital to carry at least one map of the area you are travelling through whilst hiking or bushwalking.

An alternative to using an ordinary ruler to estimate distance on a map is to use an orienteering compass that combines a ruler and compass. These are small and (besides having millimetre graduations on one edge) have the added advantage of graduations in metres and kilometres for the 1:25 000 and 1:50 000 map scale along the other edges. These graduations are particularly useful, as they allow direct distance measurements on maps at a scale of 1:25 000 and 1:50 000.

Orienteering type compass. The graduations around the edge of the compass enable direct distance map measurements.

Graduations for direct measurement from 1:50000 map

Graduations for direct measurement from 1:25000 map

Some topographic maps, and top-of-the-range tourist style maps and atlases have latitude and longitude coordinates shown on them. Coordinates taken from these maps can be used to calculate distance using degrees, minutes and seconds, although this can become quite complex. However, many such maps also use UTM coordinates, where both the coordinate grids and any distance measurements or calculations use the metric system, making life a lot easier. UTM is fully described in a later section (*Map Coordinate Systems*).

MAP DATUM

A very important detail on any map is the datum (the base lines, or 'square one') that the map uses as a reference point. A datum is, therefore, the basic framework used to define the coordinate system of the map. There are several datum in use (depending on where you are on planet earth) but each was devised by estimating the size and shape of the earth, with various systems being used to transfer the data from the curved surfaces of the globe so as to enable the production of a map on a flat surface.

With advancements in technology (particularly the introduction of GPS) a globally compatible datum was required, and the World Geodetic System 1984 (WGS84) is now universally accepted as being that globally compatible datum. A localised standard datum for mapping was adopted in Australia in 1966, and this was the Australian Geodetic Datum 1966 (AGD66). Maps based on this standard use an Australian Map Grid 1966 (AMG66; often shown on maps as just 'AMG'). To comply with the WGS84, the AMG66 has been updated to become the Map Grid of Australia 1994 (MGA94; often shown on maps as just 'MGA'). For a specific location (latitude and longitude or UTM), a map using AMG will show a particular location as being approximately 200 horizontal metres different to a map using MGA, although this will vary from place to place.

The elevation (altitude) shown will also differ, with many maps referencing the Australian Height Datum (AHD) and indicating the correction required to use alternative height datum systems. AHD is the notional 'sea level' in Australia, but as we all know, the sea is far from being a consistent height (or level) at any point on the planet.

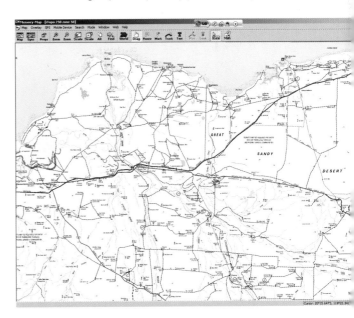

While a discrepancy of 200 metres (in the horizontal) may not sound a lot, it is at least ten times the error of a GPS reading. If any degree of accuracy is required, it is important that the GPS unit uses the same datum as the map. The datum the map is using will be clearly stated somewhere on the map, usually with all of the legend information and/or near the map title. Maps produced from about 2003 onwards will use the new datum. Fortunately, most GPS receivers have provision to accept both the earlier datum, as well as the later one and it is important to make sure that the datum being used by your GPS unit is the same as the printed format map you are referring to.

If necessary, you can convert UTM grid references from AGD66 maps to the newer MGA94 by adding 105 metres to the easting, and 190 metres to the northing.

MAP COORDINATE SYSTEMS

At this stage, an overview of how topographic maps, tourist maps, marine charts and aviation charts are constructed will prove helpful. For defining and finding locations anywhere on planet earth, some system of geographical coordinates are needed. In their simplest form, this coordinate system might be the one used in street directories. A far more sophisticated system is that of the traditional latitude and longitude, as used on marine and aviation charts. In contrast to marine and aviation navigation, most land based navigation is usually concerned with comparatively short distances. In these situations a simpler grid system can be used, and this system is known as UTM (Universal Transverse Mercator).

Street Directory Reference System

The reference system most commonly used in street directories is to divide the area covered into a number of pages, each with its own map and superimposed alpha-numeric grid. Each page is divided into a grid system, with each square on the grid representing a block of land. Along the bottom margin of the page, each square grid column is given an identifying letter and along the vertical margins each grid row is allocated a number.

Diagram 7 shows a section of a page from a typical street directory. The item of interest here is the Sports Club located on page 142, in column O, and in row 16. The club's location would be given as 'Page 142, O16'.

More formally, we would identify the name of the street directory as well as the page and grid details, so that we might end up with a reference for a boat ramp on the Albert River in Brisbane such as 'Brisway 644 D3'.

In either case, note that this system only identifies a square on the map, and therefore only identifies a block of land on the ground, not a pinpointed location. Obviously, to identify a location more specifically, a more accurate system is needed.

Topographic Map Reference Systems are more complex than a street directory, but this added complexity enables any feature to be located with great accuracy.

Latitude and Longitude

Planet earth is generally considered to be a sphere, although this not strictly true as our planet is flattened somewhat at both poles, and bulges at the equator. However, for general mapping purposes any of these anomalies can be ignored and for navigation, and mapping purposes, planet earth is divided into a vast grid system known as latitude and longitude.

Lines of latitude circle the earth horizontally and in parallel, with the equator being the line of latitude that is allocated the value of 0°, and the north and south poles being allocated the value of 90 degrees. Lines of longitude originate at a single point, the North Pole, and cross the globe in a north–south direction terminating at the South Pole. As longitude lines curve out from a single point at the North Pole and join up again at the South Pole, they are therefore furthest apart at the equator.

Lines of latitudes are numbered from the equator, in both the north and south direction. Lines of longitude are numbered from Greenwich (in England, which for historical reasons is zero degrees), extending east and west to a line on the opposite side of the planet known as the International Date Line (this is in the middle of the Pacific Ocean, and is designated 180 degrees). Diagram 8 is an easy to understand graphic representation of the globe, and shows the lines of latitude and longitude.

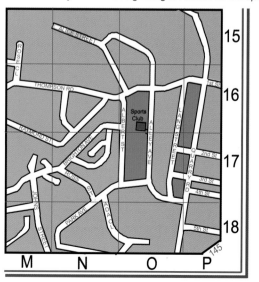

Diagram 7: Street directory illustrating the alpha-numeric coordinates system for designating locations on a map.

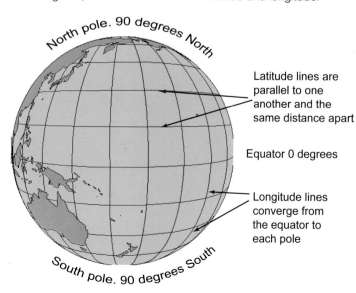

Diagram 8: A graphic representation of the lines of latitude and longitude on the World Globe.

The latitude and longitude system uses degrees, minutes and seconds to define a particular location, with minutes being 1/60 of a degree and seconds being 1/60 of a minute. Traditionally, latitude and longitude are quoted in that order, so that a location on the Bulloo River of outback Queensland would read something like latitude 27.41.26S (degrees, minutes and seconds south), longitude144.01.39E (degrees, minutes and seconds east).

Portraying latitude and longitude on the flat surface of a printed map (or on a GPS screen) creates a few problems. Globes provide a good pictorial estimate of the earth's surface, but their scale is too large (that is, they lack sufficient detail) to allow you to plan a paddling trip down a river or to guide you to your favourite fishing place on a lake shore. A flat map of the area, which shows a lot of detail and can be folded up and carried in the pocket, is more practical.

Planning ahead and being aware of approaching land configurations will ensure your trip is safe and more enjoyable.

To convert a diagram of the round surface of the earth and to transfer this information onto a flat map is a complicated process. However, think of the globe as a hollow rubber ball with the land and sea painted on it, to flatten the rubber ball onto a flat surface we would need to cut it into sections and stretch it. Because of this stretching of the surface, the land and sea areas that were painted on the ball will be distorted from the original shapes.

The same cutting and stretching method is used to portray the earth's surface on a map by using a so-called 'projection formula' (the mathematics used to convert the data from a curved surface, to a flat surface). For the

mapmaker, there are several different formulae to use, the most common being the Mercator Formula, which is the basis for nautical charts, aviation charts and most topographic and tourist maps. Gerardus Mercator was a Flemish mapmaker, one of the founding members of modern mapmaking techniques, having plied his trade in the mid-1500s.

Because lines of longitude fan out from each pole to the equator (and back again) the box grids they form with the lines of latitude (which are parallel to one another) are not square, but a distorted oblong, with the sides formed by the lines of longitude, slightly curved. For this reason, measuring distance on nautical (and aviation) charts (both of which use latitude and longitude) is not very easy. However, it is still the best system when long distances must be covered and is universally used by mariners and aviators for navigation.

Universal Transverse Mercator (UTM)

The Universal Transverse Mercator (UTM) System is a relatively new method of pinpointing a location on the earth's surface. While it is not really necessary to fully understand the UTM system to use a map with your GPS, a basic understanding will make life easier.

The UTM system divides the planet into 60 separate east-west zones, each zone being six degrees of longitude wide. These zones are numbered from 01 to 60 and start from the International Date Line, which is longitude 180°, and increases eastward. Australia is divided into six zones numbered from 50 to 56, as shown on Diagram 6. Each zone is then further divided into horizontal bands, known as Zone Designations, with each band spread north-south over eight degrees of latitude. These bands are allocated a letter of the alphabet, starting from 80° south (which is given the character 'C') and then proceeding north to latitude 84° north (which is designated letter 'X'). The characters 'O' and 'I' are not used for zone designation, in order to avoided confusion with the numbers zero and one.

UTM Zone designations for Australia.

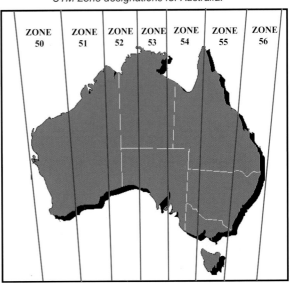

UTM can be used for land navigation and maps from 84° north to 84° south, whereas the polar regions are covered by a system known as UPS (Universal Polar Stereographic). Because the lines of longitude converge to a single point at the poles, UTM would have unacceptable errors in these regions, and the UPS system is used instead. Unless you intend to do some trekking across the Antarctic ice cap, there is little chance you would need to use UPS.

UTM is considered by many to be the preferred choice of coordinate system, as it allows coordinates to be tied directly to distance measuring and in fact, one of the major advantages of using UTM coordinates is the ease and accuracy of calculating distance. The other major advantage is that it is much simpler to use than the traditional latitude and longitude.

As well, the grid lines used to indicate UTM numbers are the same lines used to indicate the scale; this is because UTM (unlike latitude and longitude) is as much about distance as it is about location. However, at the end of the day, UTM is just another coordinate system. Like latitude and longitude, its greatest triumph is its ability to pinpoint a location on the earth's surface.

UTM was first designed in the 1940s, but it wasn't until the space age began that it became a practical proposition for navigation. UTM provides a constant distance relationship between any points on the map, whereas when using latitude and longitude the distance covered by a degree of longitude differs as you move from the equator to the poles. This is unavoidable in any system used to cover long distances on a curved surface, such as found on planet earth. However, since most land navigation is generally across a very small part of the world (at any one time) this is not a significant problem.

The key points of UTM are:
- Grid values increase from left to right, and from top to bottom.
- The system uses X, Y coordinates (Cartesian coordinates), allowing for simple mathematical calculations for distances; no special maths are needed.
- The coordinates used are decimal based – ones, tens, hundreds etc. This is unlike the latitude and longitude system which (as mentioned above) uses degrees, minutes and seconds, with each subdivision being 1/60 of the previous one.
- The coordinates are only measured in the metric system (metres and kilometres). There is no conversion possible to the miles, yards, feet and inches of yesteryear.

Referring to the illustration of the single UTM zone (Diagram 10) you will notice that in the middle of the zone there is a line of longitude called the central meridian (sometimes called the prime meridian). This is the base line from which distance measurements are taken in both the east and west directions. In the UTM system these measurements are called 'eastings' and are measured in metres from the central meridian; those in an easterly direction are positive, whilst those in a westerly direction are notionally negative numbers. However to overcome

the problem of using negative numbers, which could be confusing and lead to navigation errors, the central meridian is given an arbitrary value of 500 km (500,000 metres), which in effect adds 500 km to all readings.

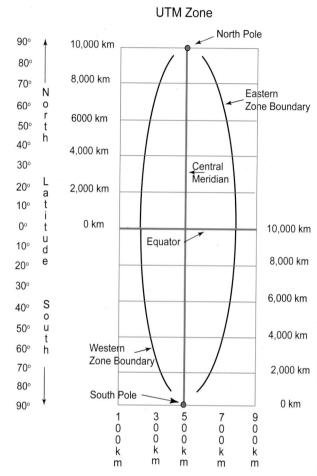

Diagram 10: A graphic illustration showing a UTM zone from pole to pole.

As an example, suppose a location is 300 km (300,000 metres) to the west of the central meridian. The nominal easting would be -300,000 metres. When 500,000 is added to this figure, the 'corrected' figure is an easting of 200,000. Since the central meridian has been assigned an arbitrary figure of 500,000, eastings are sometimes referred to as 'false eastings'.

Having given the central meridian an arbitrary figure of 500 km (500,000 metres), an easting of zero, or a negative number, will never occur since six degrees of longitude is never more than 674,000 metres wide.

Readings in the north–south direction are known as 'northings' and are measured relative to the equator. Locations in the Northern Hemisphere have their distance measured northwards from the equator (which is notionally designated as being zero). However, to avoid negative numbers for Southern Hemisphere readings, the equator is assigned a value of 10,000,000 metres, and the northing distance is subtracted from this value.

Since bigger numbers are involved in the calculations for northings compared to eastings, a northing will always be a bigger (longer) number than an easting. Many users place a '0' (zero) in front of the easting in order to make both numbers equal in length. When coordinates are given using the UTM system, the easting is always shown first, followed by the northing.

Example 1
The following data refers to a picnic area on the Wadbilliga River in southern New South Wales, (as depicted on the 1:25 000 map sheet Yowrie), UTM 55H 0733785E : 5983108N. Note that the data quoted here uses a zone designation (55H), as well as the letters 'UTM' to indicate that UTM data is being quoted.

If you use the accepted format of UTM there is no real need to use the letters UTM, and if there is no doubt as to the map that is being referred to, there is no real need to quote the zone information, although a GPS unit will always display this information.

Example 2
Diagram 11 is a section of a topographic map depicting a stretch of the Murrumbidgee River. The feature shown as 'Lime Kiln TSR' on this map has a road entrance (a t-junction) which is defined by UTM coordinates 0582136E : 6115957N. The Lime Kiln TSR (Travelling Stock Reserve) is part of a state-wide network along existing, and former, stock droving routes and provides good access to a section of the Murrumbidgee River's banks, and consequently is a popular place with anglers.

To give a UTM reference for this location to the nearest 100 metres, the grid zone designation is given first, then the easting (the large whole number on the grid line to the left of the location), and then the tenths are estimated, either by eye or by use of a scale ruler or romer protractor (more about these devices later).

In summary, UTM coordinates are made up of the following data:
- the grid zone designation
- the easting coordinate
- the northing coordinate

Together these make up the full coordinates of the location, which can only refer to a single location on planet earth.

There's more
There are a few more nitty-gritty points about UTM, none of which is crucial to your ability to operate a GPS unit, and you can skip the next three paragraphs if you wish.

Diagram 12 shows Australian UTM Zone 55 from latitude 10° (which is just north of Cape York) to latitude 44° (which is located south of Tasmania). The illustration is drawn as close to scale as possible to give an approximation of the proportions in the actual zone. By studying this diagram, you can see that the six degrees of longitude at 10° is larger than at 44°, in fact a degree of longitude measures approximately 111 km at latitude 10°, compared to approximately 79 km at latitude 44 degrees.

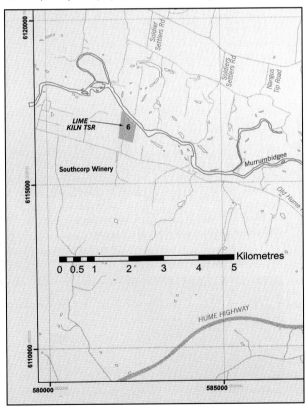

Diagram 11: Murrumbidgee River near Gundagai. This section of a topographic map illustrates how UTM coordinates are calculated for a location on the map.

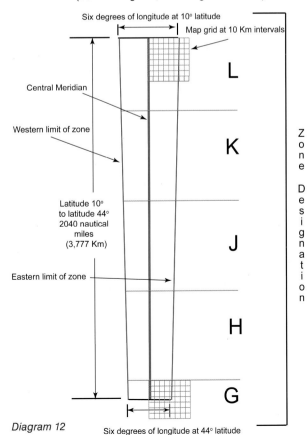

Diagram 12

A grid has been superimposed over a portion of the zone, and has grid has lines at 10 km intervals both in the horizontal direction (east–west) and the vertical direction (north–south). Note particularly that the grid is square, and not tapered like a latitude–longitude grid. Also note that the area covered by such a grid is smaller at higher latitudes in the east–west direction, but the same area for north–south directions over the whole of the zone. To put it another way, the maximum distance in metres from the western boundary of the zone to the eastern boundary is considerable less at 44° than it is at 10 degrees.

Finally, the zone boundaries are drawn as straight lines, but are in fact slightly curved, as this type of illustration is intended to show in a graphic form the application and overall layout of the UTM structure, and not portray the features to a perfect scale. In practical terms, the curvature is so small on the size of maps that are used for travel over land that it may be ignored.

Converting coordinates

To convert a UTM to latitude and longitude, or vice versa, requires either inside knowledge from the internet (search for 'UTM conversion' to get more details) or for both grids to be superimposed over the map at regular intervals. Many modern era printed maps are in this format, so it's just a case of locating the UTM grid information and following them across the map. A special device, known as a 'romer' (named after its inventor) can help do this quite quickly and keep you 'on track'. These handy devices are available from map shops and outdoor retailers; use your internet search engine to zero in on 'romer protractor' and you should find some handy outlets.

TOPOGRAPHIC MAPS

Topographic maps typically display most of the natural and man-made features of an area as well as the nature of the terrain (whether it is steep, covered in trees, covered in sand, dissected by waterways etc). Apart from these assets, a topographic map will also have detailed coordinate systems (such as latitude–longitude and UTM, as discussed earlier). These will be shown in the margins of the map, and overprinted right across the map in order to provide a clear reference as to GPS location data. Many touring style maps (such as those produced by companies such as WestPrint) will also show these details. For serious navigation in bushland and in the outback, these are the type of maps to rely on.

Contours.

Contours are the wavering lines that crawl all over topographic maps and are used by map makers to link places of equal elevation (altitude). Contours are usually drawn in groups, so that a map might show the 150 m contour, then the 160 m, 170 m etc. A less detailed

map may only show contours at 40 metre intervals, for example, 1700 m, 1740 m, 1780 m etc. In all cases, the closer the contours are together, the steeper the slope, and this has implications for all outdoor activities. A steep slope on a river bed will mean a big rapid or a waterfall, on a walking track it will involve a slower pace and more energy expenditure and on a 4WD track it will require additional driver concentration to avoid a skid or lack of traction.

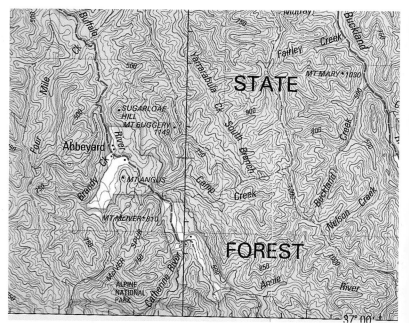

This detailed section of a topographic map illustrates the use of contour lines to show elevation.

Where there is a significant piece of high ground, the map maker may often include a 'one-off' item of elevation data. These are known as spot heights, and are often used to indicate the elevation of prominent peaks, for example, Mount Woodroffe, 1440 m (this is the highest peak in South Australia, and is just south of the SA/NT border).

The North Word.

Following on from the tradition of Nordic mapmakers from many centuries ago, the top of a map always points northwards. Despite this tradition, a 'north' arrow is always shown on a map, so that the map user can easily orientate the map for reading and navigation. Many maps (including all topographic maps) show a north arrow which has three heads; these are true north, grid north and magnetic north. True north points to the North Pole (a fixed geographic feature). Grid north is the north point as used by the map maker. It will differ slightly from true north because the map is flat, whereas planet earth is not. Finally, magnetic north points to the magnetic north pole (this moves around deep inside our planet, and maps usually show the difference between magnetic and true north as at the date of publication, as well as the predicted change over coming years).

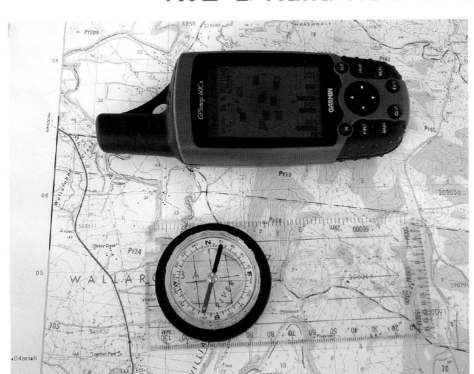

The essentials for bush navigation. Hand held GPS, Orienteering compass and topographic map.

SWITCHING ON YOUR GPS

When a GPS unit is first powered up it will usually show a map (or offer you a choice of maps) as well as things such as speed of travel, elevation and your location (GPS coordinates).

- **Coordinates** refers to the location of the GPS (as determined by satellite) and may take several minutes to be displayed; more of this in the next few paragraphs.
- **Speed** refers to the speed at which the receiver is moving, and may be shown as kilometres per hour, miles per hour or knots (nautical miles per hour; a nautical mile is about 15 per cent longer than a land mile). The different formats are user selectable.
- **Bearing** is the compass heading along which the GPS is being transported. The bearing is normally displayed via a graphic depicting a traditional compass face, with a north arrow etc.
- **Elevation** is the height above sea level, and relates to the heights and contours shown on a topographic map of the area. The Map Datum that you select from the Set-up Menu will affect the accuracy of this figure, as will the inner workings of the particular GPS unit.
- **Map display**. The map shown on the screen may need to be changed; for example, the unit may default to a standard street mapping system, and if you want some more detailed topographic maps, then you may need to use a menu setting to achieve this.

Many units display the map which was relevant to the last usage, and this may take a few minutes to roll-over to the current mapping requirement. If the unit has not been switched on for several days (this is known as a 'cold start'), then getting the initial fix may be quite time consuming. This is because the unit needs to download and analyse the 'ephemeris' data from each visible satellite. Ephemeris is the complete set of data that defines the position and status of each satellite. A cold start is sometimes referred to as a TTFF (time to first fix). GPS receivers intended for marine and aviation use may only have the latitude and longitude system installed, whilst hand-held (and in-vehicle) units will have a choice of both UTM and the latitude and longitude system. Prior to setting your GPS to either system, it is important to check what system is being used by your map as for obvious reasons you need to set the GPS to the map's coordinate system. Most maps produced in the digital era will have an overlay of both systems, mostly just around the margins of the map.

GPS units allow you to select latitude–longitude with several options, such as degrees to 4 or 5 decimal places, degrees and minutes with minutes given to two decimal places or simply degrees, minutes and seconds. Take care not to confuse these three different read-outs, as it will make a critical difference to your interpretation of the data. Showing degrees to 4 or 5 decimal places is the typical default display for many city street based GPS units.

Similarly, you may need to specify whether you want the north arrow to point to magnetic north (as in a magnetic compass) or grid north. Most users opt for grid north.

Some units require that you select a continent as a base for a satellite search, and then a particular area of that continent (for Australian usage, this will involve selecting a particular state). As well, you may need to define which time zone you are in (again, for Australian usage, this will involve selecting a particular state). Setting a time zone enables your GPS unit to update its clock from the appropriate satellite(s). Note that you cannot adjust the clock, nor the date, directly.

As an alternative to displaying maps on start-up, some units go directly to an information page that displays the current state of the system, including the status of the unit concerning its search for satellites.

• The receiver status is a very important display as this indicates that the unit has established a fix which will be either 2D (horizontal only) or 3D (length in both directions and height). Obviously, no navigation tasks should be undertaken until a reliable fix has been obtained.

The receiver status is closely related to the satellite strength displays, which indicate the satellite signals being received and used to calculate the fix. As mentioned earlier, each satellite has a unique identification number, and while four good satellite signals are necessary for a 3D fix, the receiver will also receive and evaluate several other satellite signals. The receiver will always use the best positioned satellites to give the best possible fix. The signal strength of each satellite signal is usually shown as a bar graph.

The actual position of each of the satellites in the sky is displayed, generally in circular graphic form, with the top of the display representing north. The same graphic usually displays the relative location of the sun and moon.

• Accuracy refers to the current maximum error the unit believes the fix is liable to at your location. In this case, it means that the stated location will fall in a circle of 4.7 metres radius of the unit. Accuracy may also be expressed as DOP (dilution of precision), or HPOD (horizontal dilution of precision) where the lower the figure, the greater is the accuracy of the fix.

The accuracy readings may be shown as metres or feet, depending on the system being used, and this refers to a two dimensional reading (that is, a horizontal reading). However, altitude readings are not as accurate. It has been stated that altitude error is between 150 and 200 per cent of horizontal error. For example, the 4.7 metre horizontal error would convert to 9.4 metres of altitude error. Errors of this magnitude would be unacceptable if you needed to land an aircraft in low visibility, but is quite adequate to help fix a position on the ground.

There must be a direct line of sight between the satellites and the GPS receiver for the system to operate, but this line of sight may be interrupted by heavy foliage, such as in rain forests, along river banks and in steep narrow gullies or chasms. In these conditions, if the receiver is having difficulty establishing a good fix, it is useful to know the position of the satellites. Since the position of each satellite changes rapidly, it is possible to estimate when the constellation would be in a suitable position to obtain a fix. However, poor signal recognition is less of a problem with GPS units today than it was when they first came on the market.

In any case, it is important to check the status of the signal prior to getting too involved, as this will have a major effect on the accuracy of your navigation.

LOOKING AFTER YOUR GPS

GPS units (like all other electronic gear) need some tender love and care. Some points to consider include.

• Keep the unit dry and away from dust. Having a designated 'carry case' will help protect the unit from dust and the screen from scratches.

• Don't leave it exposed to fierce sunlight for too long; placing a cloth cover over the unit will not detract from its performance.

• Remove any batteries from the unit if it is not going to be used for a reasonable amount of time.

• Don't leave the unit in an unattended vehicle overnight (GPS units are very easy to steal).

A GPS can be used in many outdoor ventures so it pays to have a good quality carry case.

MONITORING YOUR JOURNEY

As well as having an appropriate set of maps (and a GPS) with you on the journey, it is also a good idea to use the maps and the GPS to monitor your progress and to maintain a sense of place and direction. This concept is probably the most important you can adopt whilst travelling. From the outset of your journey, continually log your progress in terms of both distance covered and the approximate direction. This means that should you feel that you are 'lost', you have a basic record of how you came to this point and (in reverse) a means of back-tracking to safety.

This can be done by either annotating your maps/ atlas as you pass by particular landmarks or by making notes, either on paper (for example, in a travel journal) or if you are in a vehicle, on a PC of some kind (notebook, netbook, mobile phone, PDA etc). Many people prefer to use the waypoint facility of their GPS unit for this, and if you are on a walking trip this is certainly the easiest method to use. Waypoints can then be referred to in the reverse order to help you get back home, or to a location where your sense of place and direction kicks in and things look familiar once more.

Recording a virtual trail of breadcrumbs will help you find your way if you ever get that 'lost' feeling.

In either case, there will be a reference point to provide some checks for you. This becomes increasingly important when you leave your vehicle behind, and head off on foot for any reason.

THE MAGNETIC COMPASS AND BEARINGS

The third essential tool for navigating your way through bushland (besides a GPS and a detailed map) is a magnetic compass, even though most GPS units have an excellent compass display.

Whilst most hand-held GPS receivers do have a compass display screen, many can only indicate a compass direction when the unit is actually moving or has been moved (the speed usually needs to be about 2 km/hr or more, and the movement need only be a few metres). The unit usually calculates the compass bearing by knowing its position at the last update, and comparing that data to the data for the current position. Some units use microprocessor analysis of changes in a multi-metal crystal block as a 'high-tech' version of the magnetic compass.

In the following example, we are going to navigate to a particular point, in this case, a remote campsite in the Simpson Desert.

Assume you have a topographic map with the campsite marked on it and the correct coordinates for this feature have been entered into your GPS. The next step is to enter your starting point in to the GPS, giving the location a meaningful name, for example 'start', 'base', 'home' etc. On most GPS units you can do this by creating a waypoint and, as mentioned above, the default data when creating a waypoint is usually the current location.

If you do not intend to return to this location it is not necessary to enter the location as a waypoint, the GPS will display your position and start navigating from there as soon as you select the campsite's waypoint with the GO TO command. The GPS will then display the distance and the compass direction (bearing) to your intended destination.

However, unlike being in a boat or an aircraft, there will be many impediments to travelling in a straight line on land. In fact, it is almost impossible to travel through bushland in a straight line, and you may need to select an intermediate salient feature, such as a distinctive tree or hill, which is in the same general direction as you need to travel, and head towards this intermediate feature. Having reached the intermediate destination, you can then repeat the process as many times as necessary. Creating a fresh waypoint at each intermediate location will help get you back to base.

Suppose your course to the campsite spot is 220° and you have chosen a prominent old casuarina silhouetted against the skyline a couple of kilometres away, which is close to the 220° course you wish to travel. As you hike towards your mark, you come across a steep gully that forces you to detour a few hundred metres. After crossing the gully, continue on your way to the tree, and when you arrive at the tree take another reading of the bearing to the waypoint. This may have changed slightly, for example, it may now be 230 degrees. Now select another feature close to the correct bearing, and proceed to this new mark. Continue to use this procedure until you reach your campsite.

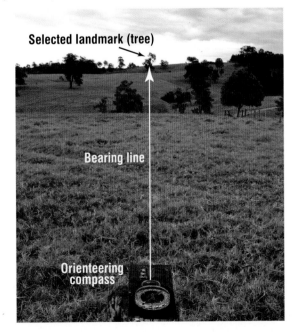

If you are travelling through open country (often the case in the outback) and/or not following any formally marked tracks, then the same techniques as used when travelling on foot apply (that is, you need to select a distinctive feature to aim for).

If the terrain is totally flat, and featureless, then some of the tricks used when navigating at sea can be useful. For example, it may be possible to take a bearing on a cloud formation, although bear in mind that clouds are mobile and do not necessarily move en masse in any one direction.

Alternatively, if the skies are clear in the direction you are travelling, often a shadow cast by part of the car (for example, a radio antenna) is enough to provide a guide. In either case, regularly check the GPS display to make sure that you are reasonably close to the course line necessary to reach your waypoint. Obviously, the aiming point will change, particularly if using a cloud formation or a shadow, and these points will change rather rapidly, so new ones will need to be selected regularly for you to stay on your intended track. Take care if you are using the sun to guide yourself, as if you 'follow the sun' all day, you will go round in a circle.

Whilst out in the bush, many people prefer to orientate their maps or GPS so that a left turn on the map appears as a left turn to the user. If you are heading north–south on a topographic map then this will not be so since north will always be the top of the map, and you are coming back down from the 'top'. You can overcome this by orientating the map so that the track you are following is pointing in the direction you are travelling. The only disadvantage with this is that all of the annotations of the map (place names, track names etc) will be upside down, or on a severe slant.

WAYPOINTS

As mentioned earlier, the ability of your GPS unit to record waypoints (significant places on your route) is one of the most useful aspects of GPS technology. As waypoints, the GPS can store the coordinates of your current location or the coordinates of any other documented locations on your route. These locations (waypoints) are then stored in memory and can be recalled when required. Using a 'Go To' function, the GPS unit can then display the distance and bearing necessary to get back to the waypoint from your current location. On most GPS units, the default data when creating a waypoint is usually the current location, although this can easily be changed.

Typically, the GPS unit will create the waypoints with names such as WP001, WP002, WP003 etc. However, you can override this basic naming system by using the 'keyboard' of the GPS (the keyboard is usually a point-to-

a-letter-and-then-press-enter system, and can be slower than creating a text message on your mobile, but it gets the job done).

For example, if you are travelling along Victoria's rugged Deddick Trail, then you might want to name the waypoints DT01, DT02 etc. Out in the Simpson Desert, you might use WAA01, WAA02 etc if you are following the WAA Line.

Having created a waypoint, each stored location will be shown with a distinctive icon on the GPS map screen.

It is a good idea to place a waypoint at each location where a significant change of direction occurs and/or where there is a road-track junction and/or where there is a significant feature (water crossing, disused mine site, viewpoint etc).

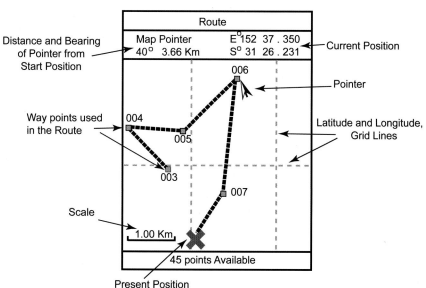

The route display page provides essential information of the current route and current position.

A series of waypoints may then be linked together to form a route (also known as a route sequence) and like waypoints, the route may be given a name and stored in memory. The route can then be navigated either in the forward direction (that is, following the route in the original direction taken when the waypoints were made) or in the reverse direction to get you back to a previous known location or back to base.

An 'event' is a more sophisticated version of a waypoint, and includes additional data such as a time and date stamp, as well as more generalised textual information.

A waypoint can also be logged as a 'POI' (point of interest) but more of this later.

MAPPING SOFTWARE

Mapping software is a very useful accessory for GPS users as it enables the user to view digital map data and to download waypoints and tracks from the GPS receiver onto a scanned map loaded into the computer, as well as entering tracks, waypoints etc directly onto the map

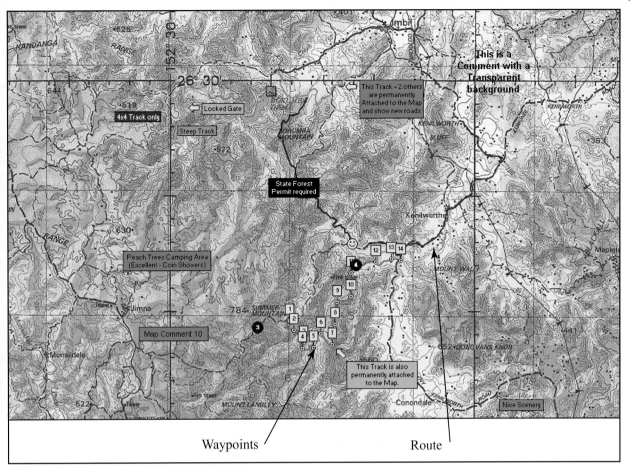

On the map, labels and comments include:
- RANDANGA RANGE
- 26° 30′
- 4x4 Track only
- Locked Gate
- Steep Track
- This Track + 2 others are permanently Attached to the Map and show new roads
- This is a Comment with a Transparent background
- KENILWORTH
- State Forest Permit required
- Peach Trees Camping Area (Excellent - Coin Showers)
- Map Comment 10
- Jimna
- SUMMER MOUNTAIN
- Monsildale
- This Track is also permanently attached to the Map.
- MOUNT LANGLEY
- Conondale
- Nice Scenery
- MOUNT WALT
- Maplet

Waypoints   **Route**

An OziExplorer map on which Waypoints, Routes and comments have been added by the user. This type of software makes planning a trip an easy task.

display on the computer. Once the map is annotated with all the new waypoints, tracks, comments and any other details, the amended map can then be printed. The new waypoints etc, which have been entered into the software, can then be uploaded into the GPS.

All of this assumes that you have the necessary map data loaded onto your PC (or similar device). Most maps produced in the modern era are available in printed and digital format.

There are a number of mapping programs available, but one of the best on the market is an Australian program called OziExplorer. This software is very easy to use and has all the features you would expect and plenty more. Another popular mapping software product with similar features to OziExplorer is Memory Map.

Maps for use with these programs may be purchased on SD cards, DVDs and CDs for uploading into a computer, or maps can be scanned and then loaded into a computer and transferred to a GPS. See *Useful Resources* at the end of the book for more details.

The ability of a mapping program to be able to accept scanned maps is quite an important feature. This ensures that maps of remote areas for which digital maps may not be available or the quality and scale is not suitable for

navigation can still be used with the software. However, take care with the map data formats as there are a number of different systems in use and not all maps work with all mapping software products.

Here is a typical scenario for planning a 4WD trip. Before the trip, work out where you want to travel (the intended route) and try to plan for an alternate route in case there are problems with your first choice (due to flooding, track closures, monsoon rain damage etc). Purchase the relevant map(s) for your trip (either on disk, SD card or via download) and then start to position the waypoints on all the road and track intersections and towns etc, attaching comments to the waypoint data where appropriate.

Following the same procedure, allocate waypoints to an alternate route in case you need another route for any reason. Then link together the waypoints that make up your planned trip to form a route. Routes and tracks are displayed on the map in different coloured lines. When you are happy with the map, upload the waypoints and events to the GPS, but remember to take a hard copy of the map(s) with you and to print the waypoint list.

Some internet sites offer free downloads of the waypoints for iconic road trips and long distance walking tracks so that most of this work has been done for you. These are normally in GPX format.

When you return from your trip, download the waypoints from the GPS to the computer. This will save any new waypoints that you may have added on the trip. Download

the tracks you recorded in your GPS during the trip and display them on the map and save everything to a file for future reference.

Planning a trip using OziExplorer is quite straightforward, as this software provides all of the mapping features mentioned above, as well as many other options. Placing waypoints on the map and saving them into a file is simplicity itself, just move the mouse cursor over the spot and click. One of the most tedious and time consuming tasks is manually imputing waypoint coordinates into the GPS receiver's memory. Using the mapping software, a couple of key strokes and any number of waypoints are uploaded to the GPS.

When you consider that there may be in excess of 100 waypoints needed in planning a relatively short trip, the value of the mapping software (even for this one feature) can be appreciated.

USING A GPS WITH A MAP AND A COMPUTER

There are many advantages to linking your GPS to a computer (or similar device), and the basic tools for doing this are a GPS unit with a USB port (USB version 2 or 3), a USB cable, a computer with a free USB port and some GPS communication software. Most manufacturers provide such software on their websites (via a free download), however there are many other software options available elsewhere on the internet. See the listing in Further Resources at the end of the book for more details.

Having made the necessary connections, and turned the GPS and computer on, the display on the GPS

should offer a range of communication options, the one designated something like 'NMEA – USB' is the one to select (NMEA stands for National Marine Electronics Association, a consortium of USA based manufacturers who established this data interface).

Apart from getting to view your GPS information on a bigger screen, there are several other advantages of the PC connection. You can download listings of waypoints for well known touring routes, as well as some long distance walking track routes. These are normally written in a GPX file format and these files can then be copied to your GPS unit, thereby saving you the effort of data entry.

IN-CAR GPS NAVIGATORS

Many vehicles have a GPS fitted as standard equipment or as an after sale accessory. These 'in-car-navigators' have inbuilt maps and extensive street directories, enabling these devices (by means of voice commands) to direct the driver to any address from the unit's maps. The standard of mapping in these units is very much based on city streets, provincial towns and regular touring routes, and when used in an off-road situation, may not be able to give directions (since there will be limited map data to refer to).

If you are seriously interested in off road expeditions, then a 4WD rated GPS unit should be near the top of your shopping list, and as mentioned earlier, the VMS4x4, Hema Navigator and the MY60T from NavMan are good choices for this task.

The VMS unit has the iTOPO range of 1:250 000 scale topographic maps, providing complete coverage of Australia. The Hema Navigator comes pre-loaded with all of the Hema outback maps (the same maps can be loaded onto the SD card of the VMS4x4), and the

NavMan unit also utilises the Hema Maps. The 4WD maps produced by Gregorys are also available in digital format, ready for transfer to a GPS. Similarly, the various state government mapping agencies now have their complete topographic map inventory available in digital format.

Regardless of the unit chosen, using a GPS for fundamental route selection is not necessarily a good move, as it is unlikely a GPS will be able to select the best (safest and most practicable) route through a particular area. So far, only the logic processes of a human brain seems capable of doing this, particularly for long and/or complex routes. As well, the verbal instructions given out will be dependent on the map used being 100 per cent accurate and up-to-date (this is not always the case).

For example, if you want to get assisted (GPS based) navigation from a minor address in the south of the Perth urban area to a similar address in the north of the urban area then the route described is unlikely to be the most efficient – but it will get you there. Navigation gets better outside of urban areas, and if you are driving from Perth to Lucky Bay (on the south coast, near Albany) for some rock fishing, then the GPS will do better than it did in the Perth metropolitan area.

Regardless of these issues, if the in-car-navigator can display the vehicle's current latitude and longitude, the vehicle's position can always be correlated to a topographical map. As well, in the case of a breakdown or other emergency, you can accurately report your position by mobile phone, satellite phone or radio.

POINTS OF INTEREST (POIs)

A POI is a feature (man-made, natural or of legal standing) that may be of interest to you whilst travelling. Examples include accommodation options, vehicle repairs and services, banking, cafe and restaurants, red light cameras, express and bus lanes, computer services, educational facilities, health facilities, recreational facilities, road hazards, road safety cameras, roadworks, school crossings, shopping facilities, speed cameras, speed limits, transportation and so on.

Your GPS mapping data will already include a substantial POI database and your GPS unit would alert you to the approach of each POI as your GPS compares your coordinate position to that of the POI.

Additional POI databases are available from several websites. Search for 'GPS POI' on your search engine for a comprehensive listing of what is available. Given the appropriate hardware connections (typically, USB ports) you would then be able to upload these to your in-vehicle GPS navigator, an easy way to augment and update the POI database. Some GPS manufacturers provide online updates of POIs (such as traffic conditions etc).

USEFUL RESOURCES

The websites listed here cover most of the major manufacturers of GPS units, as well as the Australian mapmakers who provide the mapping data used by these devices. The listing is in alphabetic order.

AFN (Australian Fishing Network): publisher of many excellent books and maps on waterways throughout Australia. *www.afn.com.au*

Explore Australia: publisher of many excellent guide books and Australia-wide touring maps. *www.exploreaustralia.net.au*

Garmin: manufacturer of hand-held GPS units. *www.garmin.com*

Geoscience Australia: publisher of the Australia-wide 1:100 000 and 1:250 000 scale topographic maps. *www.ga.gov.au*

Hema Maps: manufacturer of in-vehicle 4WD rated GPS units and publisher of many Australia-wide 4WD touring maps. *www.hemamaps.com.au*

Magellan: manufacturer of hand-held GPS units. *www.magellan.com.au*

Memory Map: developer of mapping software. *www.memory-map.com.au*

Navman: manufacturer of in-vehicle GPS units. *www.navman.com*

New South Wales Land and Property Information: topographic and touring maps. *www.lpma.nsw.gov.au*

OziExplorer: developer of mapping software. *www.oziexplorer.com*

Queensland Environment and Resource Management: topographic maps. *www.derm.qld.gov.au*

South Australian Department of Environment and Natural Resources: topographic and touring maps. *www.environment.sa.gov.au*

Spatial Vision: publisher of many excellent Victorian 4WD touring maps. *www.spatialvision.com.au*

Tasmanian topographic: Tasmap bushwalking and touring maps. *www.tasmap.tas.gov.au*

TomTom (manufacturer of in-vehicle GPS units); *www.tomtom.com*

Travel by GPS: resource site for various GPS utilities. *www.travelbygps.com*

VMS: manufacturer of in-vehicle 4WD rated GPS units. *www.vms4x4.com*

Walk GPS: Walks around Perth resource site, with GPS utilities. *www.walkgps.com*

WA Landgate: Western Australian topographic and touring maps. *www.landgate.wa.gov.au*

Westprint Heritage Maps: publisher of many excellent Australia wide 4WD touring maps. *www.westprint.com.au*

GPS SOFTWARE

The software listed here is available free from various websites around the globe, and has varying degrees of usefulness; not all of it is compatible with all GPS units.

The list is by no means comprehensive and if you search for 'free GPS software' on your internet search engine, you will find at least twice as many products as are listed here. Remember that sites and products come and go, and there may well be new sites and products for you to find, and some that are listed here may disappear.

As with much of what can be found 'free' on the internet, some caution is required before installing any of these programs. Take note of what your internet search engine tells you about each site as it retrieves them and ensure that your anti-virus software checks each download for viruses before installation.

Some of this software will have a particular GPS manufacturer's unit as the default setting and you should check the configuration of each software package before trying to use it. You may also need to set some other parameters, such as to use a USB port in preference to some other older style hardware.

3D Route Builder: build or edit GPS routes in Google Earth with altitude and time-stamp information.

AddMagMap: adds custom objects to MapSend maps.

Clew: GPS chart plotting program.

CycleAtlas: for managing track rides, mainly intended for cycling.

Earth Bridge: provides a connection between Google Earth and a GPS.

EasyGPS: create, edit and transfer waypoints and routes between a PC and a Garmin, Magellan or Lowrance GPS.

FizzyCalc: provides conversion of coordinates to various formats.

flexGPS: enables manipulation of maps used with a GPS.

G7ToWin: exchange information between a PC and Garmin, Magellan, or Lowrance/Eagle GPS.

GarFile: software tool for bidirectional transfer of waypoint, route, or trackpoint data between Garmin GPS and MapInfo.

Garmap Win: used with Garmin GPS to manage waypoints, routes, and track logs.

Garmin Communicator Plugin: browser plugin that sends and retrieves data from Garmin GPS.

GARNIX: enables transfer of data between Windows and Linux computers and a Garmin GPS.

GITMapPointCreateTrack: converts GPS logs in NMEA format created with a RoyalTek RBT3000 GPS, VisualGPS or VisualGPSce or TomTom Navigator to a track in Microsoft MapPoint.

GlobalUTM: MapInfo add-on for the supplemental display of the current cursor position in UTM coordinates in the best-matching, automatically selected / changed UTM zone.

gMapMaker: map tile downloader that supports multiple simultaneous downloads, multiple tiles per file and MSN, Yahoo, OpenStreetMap as additional map sources.

GPSBabel (Windows, OS X, Linux): manipulates and transfers waypoints, tracks and routes between units and/or popular mapping programs.

GpsDataLogger: for recording, monitoring and plotting GPS data. The program accepts NMEA GPS sentences from most GPS that connect to a USB port.

GPSMaster: mapping software that communicates with any Garmin GPS.

GPSS: in-car navigation and remote tracking demonstrations.

GPS Sway: handles all forms of latitude, longitude and UTM coordinates to convert from one to another.

GPS TrackMaker: GPS software for PC with Microsoft Windows 95 or higher. It creates, edits and deletes track logs, routes, and waypoints.

GPStrans: enables waypoint, track and route information to be exchanged with a Garmin GPS.

GPS Utility: provides management, manipulation and mapping of GPS information.

Gpx2rt2: converts GPS-tracks of *.gpx, *.mps, *.plt or *.nmea format to route files *.rt2. Software creates two route files – forward route and backward one.

ITNConv: converts a route contained in a file of Express Highway, MapPoint, or MapSource to a file used by TomTom 3, 5, 6, Go, One, and Rider, Navigon MN | 4, 5 and 6, Destinator PN, Google Earth, CartoExploreur or GPX.

LOC2WPT: provides conversion of a waypoint file (either .loc or .gpx) directly to a Mapsource file.

MAPC2MAPC: program to calibrate maps and to convert calibration files for digital maps from one format to another. Will also create Garmin Custom Maps from calibrated maps.

MapExtract: tool to extract selected pieces from large maps and load them into your Garmin GPS.

MAPKon: processes and converts tracks, routes and waypoints.

Map Maker: map editor and viewer.

MapMan: map-generating tool designed primarily for owners of Garmin GPS with mapping capability.

MapSend Lite: enables use of MapSend and Magellan maps directly on a PC.

MapSphere: mapping software for Windows.

MAPupload: program for uploading of IMG map files into a Garmin GPS.

Mapyx Quo: digital mapping program which enables connection of a GPS to a PC (manage all your waypoints, routes and tracks).

Odysseus: navigation software.

OkMap: calibrate raster maps, create vectorial maps, display simultaneously raster maps and vectorial data, import digital data, create waypoints, routes and tracks.

POI databases: these covers POIs (Points of Interest) around the country and are available from several websites (search for 'GPS POI' on your search engine for a comprehensive listing of what is available). Typically, you would then upload these to your in-vehicle GPS navigator. See the main text for more details.

POIConverter: converts POIs, routes and tracks between selected formats.

POI_DB_extractor: extracts MapSend POI database.

PoiEdit: manages POI files from a PC and saves/loads them to/from a mobile device.

RoadNav: in-car navigation system.

sendMap: uploads maps to a GPS.

ST_to_GPS: upload and create routes from Microsoft Streets & Trips to a GPS.

S&T Keys: Hotkeys for Microsoft Streets & Trips. S&T Keys simplifies the usage of Microsoft Streets & Trips for GPS navigation use.

TOPO_creator: creates custom Topo maps compatible with MapSend/MMO.

TOPO_extractor: extracts topographic info from MapSend's BLX files.

TopoFusion: GPS Mapping software.

Track-Album: download GPS tracks and view them in 3D in Google Earth.

Trackan: processes an existing track to provide interesting statistics such as total ascent, total descent, moving average speed.

TritonRMP: creates custom raster maps compatible with Triton units and Vantage Point software.

VisualGPS: displays all satellites that are in view.

Waypoint Stitcher: combines two or more GPX or LOC waypoint files into a single file.

WikimapiaGPS: connects Wikimapia and a GPS.

WinGDB3: companion program to Garmin's MapSource performing various conversion and filtering functions.

GPS HARDWARE

The number of different GPS devices (and accessories) available on the market seems to increase every year, making it harder and harder to decide which unit will best suit your needs. To make your purchase easier, start your product browsing at the manufacturer's website, and then (if necessary) move over to the local supplier's website, taking note that not all overseas products are available in Australia.

As well, take care if you place your order with an overseas based supplier, as you may not get Australian maps as standard equipment.

Key things to consider when purchasing a GPS unit include screen size, maps supplied as standard, optional maps, map updates, memory size (500Mb is regarded as the minimum by many users), an SD card reader and USB connectivity (hardware and software). If you opt for a built-in unit (as opposed to the free-standing units described below) then you would normally get a larger screen size than the sizes quoted here.

So as to make life a little easier for you, here is a basic run-down of what is available in alphabetic order of the manufacturer's name . . .

GARMIN

GARMIN has by far the largest range of GPS devices, and groups its products in categories such as automotive, aviation, fitness, marine and outdoors.

In Vehicle:

The in-car devices are dominated by the extensive Nüvi Series, and these provide a wide range of hardware options to choose from; at least one for every situation and user need. The basic end of the range is represented by the **Nüvi 40**, and the top of the range is the **Nüvi 3790LMT** and there are over a dozen models in the range.

Garmin has downloadable map options including TOPO Australia and New Zealand on micro SD Cards that feature: topographic terrain contours at 20 metre intervals, tracks and outback trails, national parks, caravan parks and more.

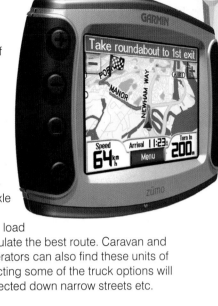

Motorcycle usage is covered by the **Zûmo** Range, and typical of the demands made of GPS in the motorbike world, these units are sturdier than the average GPS, along with robust waterproofing and dustproofing.

The truck focussed units allow the user to enter gross weight, axle weight, height, length and width, as well the load being carried, to calculate the best route. Caravan and large motorhome operators can also find these units of great benefit, as selecting some of the truck options will prevent you being directed down narrow streets etc.

Hand Held:

Outdoor usage of a GPS comes with the need for lightweight units with good sized screens and a long battery life. Being WAAS enabled helps when the user is under a rainforest canopy in south-west Tasmania, or amongst the tall timber of the Victorian high country.

Having a strong colour screen display is also a factor in a completely outdoor setting (sun glare can be a problem in the outdoors) and all of the factors mentioned here are standard features in the **GARMIN eTrex** range. There are three models in the range and the **eTrex 30** features a barometer.

Other models include the **Montana, Rino, Dakota, Oregon, GPSMAP** and the innovative wrist model **Foretrex**. These models come with micro SD cards to load the various map options.

HEMA

In Vehicle:

HEMA are renowned as the leading Australian producer of 4WD and general touring maps, and their GPS unit (the **Hema Navigator** – also known simply as **HN5i**) continues this great tradition with an amazing bundle of maps as standard equipment. The Hema Navigator has a 5 inch screen, and an easy to use interface that will have you an expert in no time. The maps supplied as standard includes street mapping (for Australia and New Zealand), the complete collection of Hema maps (4WD and touring), as well as a complete set of 1:250 000 topographic maps for Australia. There is also access to a wide range of aftermarket maps, such as the NSW 1:25 000 and 1:50 000 scale topographic maps.

There are three options in this unit – all come inclusive with the GPS for On and Off road navigation.

Street Nav Preloaded with the latest Australia and New Zealand street data. Also includes CAMPS 6 Australia Wide site locations and HEMA outback 4WD tracks.

4WD Nav Preloaded with HEMA 4WD and Touring Maps and Aust TOPO 1:250 000 map. Also includes HEMA Ezi Ozi interface to easily harness the power of OziExplorer.

Topo Nav Preloaded with HEMA 4WD and Touring Maps and Aust TOPO 1:250 000 map. Also providesaccess to Australia's widest range of high resolution topo maps and marine charts.

Along with VMS (see below) Hema are the leaders in outback GPS mapping.

MAGELLAN

In Vehicle:

The Magellan **RoadMate** series of GPS provides a good range of options for vehicle based navigation, including a vehicle mounting kit and a 7 inch screen. Providing that you purchase the unit from an Australian supplier, then the unit includes full street mapping of Australia, along with the option to purchase a range of Hema maps, as well as topographic maps covering every state.

Hand Held:

The **Explorist** Range provides a good choice of handheld units models GC, 310, 510,610 & 710, with screen sizes of up to 3 inches, and a 16 hour battery life. They come standard with topographic maps 1:250,000 covering all of Australia are provided as standard gear, as well as a complete range of street maps.

There are detailed Summit Series maps available 1:25 000 Australia/ New Zealand as well as each individual state.

Some users might prefer the **Triton** Range, as these are much smaller (and lighter) than the Explorist units.

NAVMAN

In Vehicle:

NavMan's Range of In vehicle GPS units for Around Australia and Off Road starts with the **EZY** Range, moving up to the larger MY units, with the **MY ESCAPE** units being at the top of the range.

The EZY Range has 4.3 inch screens, and includes all of the features and alerts that we have become accustomed to whilst on the bitumen, as well as up-to-date street mapping.

The MY Range features a 5 inch screen, as does the MY ESCAPE Range. The latter units also have some additional

handy features such as being able to select 'large vehicle' as the vehicle type (handy for caravans, and other long rigs), as well as being dust and vibration proof (handy for all those outback tracks).

Designed for drivers of Light Commercial Vehicles, those towing a boat or caravan, Four Wheel Drivers andmotorhome owners, the Navman MY ESCAPE GPS features Large Vehicle Assist ensuring you avoid roads that are not suitable for your vehicle size or weight. The built-in Hema 4WD Tracks takes you off road, camping or adventuring with just one sat nav device whilst Lonely Planet Travel Guides and Scenic Routes works as your local travel guide while on holidays.

The well-known HEMA 4wdmaps are a standard feature on the **MY ESCAPE** and **MY75T** units. The same maps are available to purchase as an optional extra for the **MY85XLT**, **MY80T**, **MY65T** and **MY60T** models.

PRONAV

In Vehicle:
ProNav GPS unitsinclude the **ProNav PNN200** and the **PNN300** that utiliseNavevo's navigation softwareto be able to enter acaravan or Light Commercial Vehicle's vital statistics including weight, axle weight, height, length and width, as well the load being carried; this allows the unit to calculate the best route to ensure you are not confronted with roads, or obstacles not suitable for your vehicle or your goods.The units also feature an FM transmitter so that you can hear the navigation instructions via the vehicle's sound system;a real benefit in the nosier environment found in trucks. Committed to development, Navevo have worked closely with its own network of testers and drawn upon feedback to continually enhance the ProNav with better data, faster processing and improved calculations. This device is now available as a first to market solution in Australia and the USA.

TOMTOM

In Vehicle:
The original tom-tom was a drum used by indigenous people of North America as a means of communication. The modern day TomTom is represented by some snappy GPS units covering several product ranges. Updated maps can either be purchased as Micro SD cards or downloadable from the TomTom website.

The **GO** series are designed for car usage, and increase in sophistication (and screen size) as you move up through the range to the **VIA**, **XXL** and **XL** units. The **PRO** Range is intended for light commercial vehicle use, and

as well as a 5 inch screen, features all of the usual vital data entry parameters (such as height, width, length etc.) so that you don't get into any awkward situations.

Hand Held:
For more personal use, TomTom has a sports watch with GPS capability. These are mostly pitched at those of us that enjoy activities such as orienteering; however having a watch with in-built GPS is very handy for any traveller in the outdoors.

TomTom also produces an application for use with the iPhone and iPad that can be easily downloaded via the iTunes store. The application features a broad range of TomTom features that can be easily updated and taken with you wherever you go.

VMS

In Vehicle:
VMS units are pitched at the 4wd market, and boast Australia-wide street mapping, as well as the iTOPO range of 1:250 000 scale topographic maps, pre-loaded, providing complete coverage of Australia in handy detail. The 4wd maps produced by Gregory's are also pre-loaded, and these provide good coverage of much of Australia's outback including camping areas and petrol stations. Various state government mapping agencies now have their complete topographic map inventory available in digital format; for example, Victoria is covered by two data files (Victoria East and Victoria West) that cover the entire state at a scale of 1:25 000, and these are also available from VMS on a memory card.

The VMS Touring **700HD** is in every way a revolution. It's the first portable Off Road Navigator to have a 7 inch High Definition screen. It's also much more powerful and comes bundled with all of the latest street andoff road maps.

Other portable models include the **Touring 430**, **Touring 500S** and the **Touring 600**. Screen size ranges from 5-8 inches, and a touch screen interface provides ease of use for driver and/or passenger.

Hand Held:
VMS also produces an award winning application for use with the iPhone and iPad that can be easily downloaded via the iTunes store. The application features a broad range of VMS features that can be easily updated and taken with you wherever you go.

INDEX

LOCALITY	DESCRIPTION	COMMENTS	LATITUDE	LONGITUDE

MAKE TRAX

LOCALITY	DESCRIPTION	COMMENTS	LATITUDE	LONGITUDE

LOCALITY	DESCRIPTION	COMMENTS	LATITUDE	LONGITUDE

LOCALITY	DESCRIPTION	COMMENTS	LATITUDE	LONGITUDE

LOCALITY	DESCRIPTION	COMMENTS	LATITUDE	LONGITUDE

LOCALITY	DESCRIPTION	COMMENTS	LATITUDE	LONGITUDE